This second book from a promising new poet thrums with dark disaffection with suburbia, societal "norms," and an American Dream that has become a nightmare. Packed with pungent images and creative, high-octane wordplay, the poems feature unforgettable lines like "Spring sun has chucked back its head /and hocked little wads of green on the blood-frosted earth / It's so beautiful I can't even see it." This author likes to turn things, then turn them again, inside out. Sometimes sardonic, sometimes apocalyptic, the poems grab you, pull you in close, then leave you with a gut punch message leavened by humor and a sense that, in spite of the bitter everything, love still matters, and might be enough.

> Rebecca Foust, former Marin Poet Laureate and author of *YOU ARE LEAVING THE AMERICAN SECTOR: Love poems* (Backbone Press 2024)

In Melina Cohen-Bramwell's *Nevada*, childhood is a broken promise and the future is not guaranteed. Nevada is a metaphor, a state of mind, something to survive and—if you're lucky—escape from. With the edgy irony and honesty of youth, unapologetically visceral and vivid, *Nevada* is painted with a seductive darkness tinged with hope, impossible to turn away from.

> Thea Hillman, author of *Intersex [for lack of a better word]* and *Depending on the Light*, both published by Manic D Press

Melina Cohen-Bramwell's *Nevada* evokes the scorching desert air suffused with tender heartbreak. The spare, beautiful language glitters with internal rhyme, and loneliness, in this volume, lives in tandem with hope. Reading *Nevada* aloud to myself, I felt the words asking readers to believe – and to remember what belief has felt like – while chiding us for undue trust. *Nevada* summons the paradox that lives in each human heart, and it takes a writer like Cohen-Bramwell to break open this paradox and lay it bare.

> Dr. Philippa Kelly, dramaturg/educator, and author of *The King and I*

Gnashing Teeth Publishing
242 East Main Street
Norman AR 71960
http://GnashingTeethPublishing.com

Printed in the United States of America

ISBN 978-1-966075-21-9

Gnashing Teeth Publishing First Edition

Nevada

Table Of Contents

Nevada

The land never ends around here

On all sides
it just

continues

unbreaking

The only waves
heat off parched earth

Little schisms   lead to just more land lower down

The heat

breathes for the ground

Breathe for me

In

Out

The Villain of the Story

Count Brightside swims in a child's lake
You'll catch him at an uncle's wake
or under red hats   spitting in red dirt
in front of the Family Dollar

He calculates the dose you score   a little too heroic
and whoops   there's one less of you
rattling at the cage of the zoo
when vacationers next take a wrong turn through your town

The picket-fencers hand him back to the can-denters
cause they know he likes to drown
people who swim with him too long

You think
the Norms and Trinas don't need him
Over the hills   the mountains painted fall gold
it's all bright sides where their license plates drive home
with their aspen drops of foliage
It must be so bright it's blinding

Pill-ow Princess

1.

Gina walks with swagger

The boys all staring at her

like there's nothing else to look at

There's not

but she doesn't let that get her down

She'll compete with dust all day and win

and only lets them stick it in

if they pay for the mourning after

2.

Gina has friends in high places

and they're happy to take you there

Pay her for a tip

and if she doesn't touch yours

she'll tell you where to find your own euphoria

What you can't get in school corridors

You can find behind the 7/11

It's not heaven

but it'll do in a pinch

3.
Gina has a house with 70s wood paneling
where you can stay forever
as long as you're having fun

Gina has a mom and a grandma
but they don't talk to her anymore

No one cares about a whore
She says
she's an entrepreneur
She says
She's a small business
and the other kids love it
They hang out all day

How else can a girl make friends
The party never ends but the friends
come and go
back to school or
their Dad's house if their Dad isn't coming
over soon to pay
Gina a visit
she's got the digits of half the men in this town
and a GED she got last week
for going down on the test administrator

4

she doesn't mind if you want to take her
for a fool
What else is there to do here
We've been bored since we were born

It's Like Cigarettes

I mean everyone knows
you're not supposed to be a teenage hooker

But where's the thrill in every sunrise
knowing you'll be alive when it sets
I wanna see the horizon of life and death
Nothing's more powerful than riding
a guy who knows he shouldn't be there

She runs her hands through bleached hair
and wipes her nose

We all crave a life that curls our toes
a little blood so you know it's not a dream

Blue Balls

Officer Krum likes to taste a little blood

He likes it rough   and he can dish it but he can't take it
says Gina

He likes to tell her about all the mean things he did
on the mean Fernley streets
and under her sheets

he just wants her to say good job

Why Not Live Like This Forever if I'm Laughing Too

Here's someone's only daughter

doing a line of Vicodin off the table in her baby-blue thong

Here's her ass peeking out of her pajama pants

milky white streaked with electric powder

that I'm railing through tips from the ice cream parlor

dusted in azure

We grew up together

and we all let this happen

this slow emptying

this trickle that becomes a torrent

while you're asleep at night

We all let this happen

and we forgot what it was like

before we started laughing at this joke

and pretty soon we'll have said it often enough

that we won't be joking anymore

A Growing up How-to Guide

Pt. 1 A Perfect Childhood

no one hears you scream
it's only inside
no one believes you
you can't look in their eyes
all you want is to sleep
but you can't find the dark
all of your little friends
are fucked up in the park
all your terrible dreams
are slowly coming true
if you scream with a smile
nobody hears you

Pt. 2 Paranoid Dementia

Two kids I once knew
now he said she said in the living room
None of our business but the voices boom too loud
to pretend   at the party's end   they're
at it again and again and again

I wanna fuck you when you're drunk
I wanna fuck you when you're sleeping
'cause you'll be waking up with nothing in your head

Remember the good old days when we weren't addicts
and you weren't mean
remember those days when we wanted to be seen
when we were so young
so little   no one could have gleaned
the future from our burning eyes

Senioritis

The party's over at Gina's house

Someone's in jail

and another snatched back into the clutches
of the nuclear family

or shipped off to another state

I'm still here waiting for someone to come
pick me up
take me home and ground me

kicking gray snow at the ragged brush out front
the rush is over but I'm still right outside her door

you're the only one who comes over anymore
just you and the tricks

All-American High School Heartthrob

Norman Rockwell fell from wherever they kept him
and got trapped in this hell
the dream he helped sell is wandering through the desert
living off cactus water
imagining trees or a drugstore jackpot

You don't believe it for long
but the throngs of itchy teens
filing in and out the double doors
says enough people will throw in their last couple chips
to keep up the facade

I'm so invisible here you'd think I was the wind
I could do anything   and people wouldn't even notice I was gone

We Can Survive Anything

If you're the wind I'm the dirt

They love us for fun when they're done
they think they can shut the door
and hide the roar and whip
the spinning dust cloud outside
from their delicate eyes

But nature is perpetual
Every square notion
of treadmill forward motion
law-abiding and suburbia-safe
citizens with dishes in the sink and
everything on black
will collapse

and we'll still be here

everyone's running for it   but no one can get there
and they'll wish they knew what we knew

Safety Net

I haven't been to school in a month

Gina says school is for suckers
I can always be a trucker or she can set me up
with a nice cushy job in the underground
Benefits are shit but prescriptions are covered

Beneath the blind eye of Officer Lover
our futures are looking bright

She blows me more fairy dust
lets day enter night
and night after night
the nights now are endless

The Scenic Route

The scent of diesel
sun-softened tires and
truck stop cheeseburgers
is my alarm

I self-harmed my way to a new part of town last night

Haven't swung around since I was eight
to watch the trucks pull in and out

Now it's too late to hitch a ride
somewhere far away

where the air reeks of pine

Somewhere the hike down the highway doesn't end
redolent of vomit

crusted shoes
Back home

Mama's singing the blues

Get your shit together or get out

A Victim of the Unemployment Crisis

The ice cream shop politely informed me I was fired
this afternoon as I wandered by
busy fighting a haze but they want me to know
they haven't seen me in days
or is it months

and the moms and toddlers   tweens and fathers
lined up inside don't tolerate this kind of behavior
Yes   it's a shame for all the good kids to see
a former good kid like me
as if the rest aren't idling in the parking lot   waiting for a light

but I can abide   I'm riding the skyline
If they had the time   there was something I came down here for
Yeah   I'm living with that whore
Go ask my mother yourself what happened

Tripping at the Speedway

A family outing
to watch adrenaline
power ambitious young men through
the carnage of four-wheeled glory

These sensation seekers get spectators
Every few weeks real families
who brought up their kids
in Nevada's certified worst place to live
clamor to gawk at the down-home glamor of a little rough and
tumble

They're here to pick a winner but they don't know
losers have all the fun
Me and Gina can put on a show like you've never seen
run up speeds that sound obscene
and feel it the next day

Pick your poison
She says
She brought a buffet
We're not racing anything but ourselves
just to make sure no one gets anywhere

Gina Had a Dream This Morning

A desert sunrise
a spiky weed
on fire but not burning
a classic
Telling her   heed this warning
This is your chance
The strip malls and the sky in dance

Casino lights
and gunfights on the highway
aren't the only sparks
Something's in you that can start
at any time

Always half awake
Always peeking
Pick a side
Plug the leaking

So she tried to plug her mouth but
it all poured out

When you puke that's when it really kicks in
It's not that she said
I didn't see it
but she insisted it was there

An Official Wellness Check

A little fluid for some information
On Wednesday they're raiding the gas station

The boys on the west side cut their pills with pesticide
It gets you fucked up in the bad way

You want more then give more away

A trip inside for the inside scoop
I'm so lucky you keep me in the loop

Your friend's always here   what's the deal with that

Big boy you've got nothing to worry about

Slot Money-Shot

A silver flood at Walgreens

Me and Fernley's pillow queen
giddy
scooping it off the floor

Hold onto it for me

With that little wink I can't say no

but the back of my head knows how far it would go

Three and a quarter pills
Or maybe the leftover for some groceries

Floorboard Treasure

Put it somewhere I can't find it and change my mind
We don't need it for anything
I work all the time

I want you to plant a dream for us
I want to imagine it grow
Think of all the places we could go
that would be nothing like here

Snow coddled mountains
always edging out of reach

Not far enough
I want California
Sand castles and beach tans

I want to see the woods
We can write our own fairy tale
You can be little red riding hood
no wolves allowed

Hide it
We can't spend it till we're clean
One day we'll see the ocean
One day we'll be the trees
and breathe

Attack of the Panic

Spring sun has chucked back its head
and hocked little wads of green on the blood-frosted earth

It's so beautiful I can't even see it

My eyes are too busy prying for
something that hits like a brick to the chest

Like an elephant
sitting on your
throat always open for business
but never letting out your secrets
Gina maybe

we just need to talk more
or less   what I was saying
is maybe we talk just enough
but not about the right things   maybe

tonight we could just breathe for a minute
with our diaphragms
like 4-6-1 and imagine

what you and I could have become
in the life they wanted for us

Daddy's Little Miracle

I wanna keep this one
His daddy's a Krum
so he can be safe
or something like it

Gina's gonna break the news
She's gonna break out of here
She gonna start a new life
She's gonna cold-turkey fear
No more dipping into the sugar
No more tomorrow nights
spent today

But when the officer comes around
it's with a smile
that can't wait to eat you up
and in the back room there's drumming on the walls
and chanting

Gina's on TV

They said it was an overdose   but she had
nightstick-shaped bruises on her back
They displayed her for all to see at the freeway theater
a starring role in the ditch
A warning to the next stuck-up bitch
who imagined she had a right to her own life

Glowing in the neon lights
her crimson halo
Easier to wipe
the dust off the windshield
Letting it ride's not worth the suspension
or the threat to the pension
or the ticked-off wife

They laid her down with the tumbleweeds
rolled her across the cracking earth
No one misses the absent
No one cries for the dirt

Cry   Bloody

The tumbleweeds and the ciccadas
                              scream
        The silt blurred walls and all
                              18 wheels of every vehicle
running down
                    the roads
that walled us in this prison
                         all of us in this prison
scream and scream
                    and pound the edges of my head
I'm not out of my bed
                    I'm not up off the ground
                              at the funeral
                    her mother and grandmother
are screaming

        and there isn't a sound loud enough
to hear

The Breeze Is Forever
The Dirt Is Forever

Gina's floorboard treasure unearthed in a grocery bag
The Greyhound teller's getting mad
How many quarters do you have

I'm going to Mendocino
I'm gonna see trees so big they blot out the sky
water that isn't running down a mother's face
in a dusty newspaper stand

can't follow me across state lines anymore
I'm gonna take my hands to the shore and
my head to the leaves
and the endless land behind me I will fly
whistle and whip hair into eyes
I will live in the sky
with Gina

Nothing can end if you don't let it
Nothing is here
I have to try and fear only my memories
I have to try to buy Gina's new life with her bag of luck
I already don't remember any of it

I have to see if it's everywhere

About the Author

Melina Cohen-Bramwell he/him, dropped out of high school to join the circus but, as it soon became clear, was far better suited to a life of hermitage. He now communicates with the outside world primarily through scraps of paper covered in discarded lines that float out the window on breezy afternoons— and the occasional cohesive manuscript slipped in single pages under the door. If you wander about when the moon is high and the wind blows at just the right timbre, you might catch a glimpse of him darting in and out of the shadows in the San Francisco Bay Area. He also just so happens to be a biracial, gender-queer, spoonie. His play, *Please Don't Slow Me Down*, had its world premiere at Little Boxes and Space 1308 in 2025. His play One of the Good Ones, received a reading in 2022 at Theatre Battery and another in PlayGround SF's 2024 Free Play Festival. His play AL'S CULT premiered at PlayGround SF's 2025 Free Play Festival. His book, Bar Fights with Sad Kids, is available from Finishing Line Press or an internet commerce site near you.

www.ingramcontent.com/pod-product-compliance
Lightning Source LLC
Chambersburg PA
CBHW051337120626
46547CB00016B/2588